THE ABC OF RUGBYY

is a guide to help you enjoy the World Cup even more. (If you are, however, buying this excellent and very reasonably priced volume after the World Cup, it will be equally valuable).

Delight at the true Rugbyisms that you now see in a new light. Learn a little about those who surround the sport.

As they say in this, the delicate game — forget the rules, let's kick off!

GREN

Published by Western Mail Books

Thomson House, Havelock Street, Cardiff CF10 1XR
Telephone: 01222 583583/223333
Registered Number 46946 England

Written and Drawn by

Gren Jones O.B.E.

Designed & Typeset by

Prestige Guides Pre-press, Western Mail & Echo Ltd.

Printed by

WME ColourPrint Division, Western Mail & Echo Ltd.

Bound by

Stephens And George Ltd

Distribution

University of Wales Press.

British Library Cataloguing-in-Publication Data.

A catalogue of this book is available from The National Library of Wales and The British Library

ISBN: 1-900477-12-2

ALL BLACKS.

Very big hairy men from New Zealand very popular as tourists. They could become a lot more popular if they'd lose a bit more often.

ASSASSIN.

There's at least one in every team, usually the hooker or second row. They run about a lot and get over excited if they don't get their hands on the ball for a while.

ALTERCATION.

What they call a punch-up at Harlequins.

AUSTRALIANS.

Australians are people who always seem to be at every top game as supporters, justifying their presence by wild claims of ancestry. Hence you will find many Aussies supporting Ireland, Wales, Scotland and England.

BLIND SIDE.

This is the back row position furthest away when your scrum half is putting the ball in. A great position if you enjoy throwing the odd sneaky punch because the ref is usually unsighted fussing about watching the scrum half.

BLINDER.

As in 'Yewer 'avin a blinder killer boy'. A term of encouragement often heard in Welsh Rugby.

C IS FOR...

CENTRE.

The positions between the wingers, there are two of them, usually one is all flair, guile, and ghosting while the other always wants to smash his way through brick walls.

COACH.

The man who has the responsibility for developing the club's style of play, tactics and approach to each game. This is instilled into the players until they actually get on the field of play, and forget all about it.

TODAY WE DO DRIFT DEFENCE, AND HOW TO GET AN AGENT.

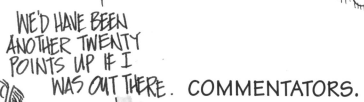

WE'D HAVE BEEN ANOTHER TWENTY POINTS UP IF I WAS OUT THERE.

COMMENTATORS.

These are usually smart arse ex-internationals who pretend they can understand what's going on out there on the pitch. While not exactly disguising that they feel they are still capable of playing better than that mob on the field.

COMMITTEE.

Rugby is run by committees, it's almost impossible to be a member of a rugby club without being asked to join one committee or another - however, keep refusing.

DRIFT DEFENCE.

A situation where the defending team are running about behind the point of attack hoping they don't have to actually tackle anyone.

DROP KICK.

This is when the player allows the ball to touch the ground split seconds before his boot makes contact.

If he accidentally kicks the ball before it bounces he will tell everyone he wanted to punt it!

DROPPED.

If a player finds his name missing from the team sheet he is said to have been dropped. This usually comes about because of a recent string of poor games or he has been caught in bed with a selection committeeman's wife.

The player will of course put the story about that being dropped was due to his style of play being considered far too progressive for this club.

E IS FOR...

EARLY BATH.

An euphemism for getting sent off. Many a Welsh player, after being sent off and finding himself in a lonely empty dressing room, has drained the hot water from the visiting team showers and spread dollops of winter-green liniment on the inside of the ref's Y fronts. Ensuring the visit by the opponents and ref will always be remembered unpleasantly.

ENGLAND.

An emerging rugby nation, one of the few national sides to still have positions such as 'steand orff'.

Some English clubs have letters on their shirts instead of numbers. This is because some English club players still haven't mastered counting yet.

EXPENSES.

What players used to get lots
of before the game went
professional.

IS FOR..

FORWARD PASS.

Something your side never
does but the opposition are
always doing it - but the ref
doesn't notice.

OOPS
DEARIE
ME!

13

FRONT FIVE.

Usually the ugliest members of the team with hardly a
front tooth between them. They are a sort of team within
a team, each looking after the other.

A good looking un-scarred front five member is
usually someone having his first senior game
straight out of the youth.

FULL BACK.

The full back wears a number 15 on his shirt and is usually the poseur of the team. He screams 'my ball' when there are no opposition players thundering down upon him when he fields a high ball. If there are, he shouts 'your ball' as he runs back to hide toward his goal line - a move he says that has something to do with tactical awareness.

GARY OWEN.

A ball kicked high and roughly in the direction of the opponent's goal line (anywhere will do actually). This tactic is specifically designed to half-kill who ever is stupid enough to try to catch it, while all opposing psychopaths, assassins and all round nutters juggernaut their way towards the catcher in the hope of redefining bodily contact.

GROINING.

A delicate little infringement so beloved of front row forwards. Often used at line outs and mauls.

GRUBBER KICK.

A showy kick often used by the flaxen haired type of outside half, who often tries to impress the touch-line talent by delicately tapping a low trajectory kick which should find a gap and eventually wobble into touch.
If this fails the winger is blamed for not having read the move - he was expected to chase, pick up and score.

H IS FOR...

OOPS, SORRY!

HACK.

A loose kick at the ball which old experienced players combine with a follow through in the direction of the nearest opposition knee-cap or shin.

HALF TIME.

A break after forty minutes of the game to give the coach time to question what the hell his players are doing.

HOOKER.

In rugby circles this is, of course, a position, not a profession. Hookers spend most of their time in the warmth and dark cosy set scrum. It's hardly strange therefore that when he is suddenly subjected to bright sunlight when the scrum breaks, he behaves in a nervous frightened manner. This disorientation makes him extremely violent to any nearby player not wearing a shirt similar to his.

INJURY.

Something players feign when
the mid-summer Annual County
Sevens Tournament is due.

INSIDE HALF.

Usually little and bandy-legged,
this player just can't stop
chattering.

He's the one who puts the ball
into the set scrum. As he waits
for its release he considers if he
should make a break himself or
give the ball out - this decision
often depends on how much of a
psycho the opposing flanker is.

INTERNATIONAL.

A game for which you can't get a ticket unless you get invited on a hospitality deal or are related to someone on the committee.

THAT'S PROBABLY ENGLAND IN BLUE!

JAPANESE.

Clever little players -
their shortage of
height has never been
a problem in the world
of international rugby.
In a recent game
several of their
opponents, the All
Blacks, returned to
their dressing room
with nasty cauliflower
knee-caps.

JENKS.

The world's greatest kicker; often copied, never bettered. This boy can back-heel a conversion from the touch line with a force ten gale blowing against him.

I'M NEVER SURE IS HE JINKING OR STAGGERING?

JINKING.

A run in which the player moves in all directions hoping he can off-load the ball before anyone tackles him.

K IS FOR...

KAMIKAZE.

This is a tackle involving a twenty stone marauding second row psycho going flat out for the line, when he's targeted head-on by a nineteen stone all bone and muscle assassin, these kamikaze tackles often register on the Richter scale.

KICK OFF.

In the lower reaches of rugby union this often means when the ref, players and touch judges are ready, often fairly near to the time on the actual match posters.

OK. LIGHTS, CAMERA, ACTION – RIGHT ROLL IT!

"THEY **KNOW** I CAN'T WEAR PUCE!"

PUGH & CO

KIT.

Used to be dignified, pretty coloured hoops, now it's often garish diagonal, zig zag lines with logos everywhere.

LEGEND.

A name given to any player who has been banned from every hotel he has stayed in on the club's Easter tours.

LOOSE HEAD.

This is the name given to the chap in the front row nearest to the scrum half when putting the ball in. He prefers playing loose head to tight head because he doesn't like the dark.

LOUD MOUTH.

The one you always seem to be sitting next to while watching a local derby.

GO FORTH AND MULTIPLY REF!

M IS FOR..

I'M NEVER QUITE SURE REF - AM I RUCKING OR MAULING?

MAUL.

When players are on their feet while trying to punch each other. This is known as a maul. When players are on the ground trying the same thing, this is known as a ruck.

MILLENNIUM STADIUM AT CARDIFF ARMS PARK.

Quite simply the greatest stadium in the world where the 1999 Rugby World Cup finals will be staged.

MOTIVATION.

Players sometimes need to be motivated - usually this is done by the coach and varies from the 'now get out there and be prepared to die for your country' to the 'you're a great fairy Jones - now get out there and prove me wrong.'

NOW GET BACK OUT THERE AND HIT HELL OUT OF HIM !

COACH

IS FOR..

YOU'RE NOT RELEASING !

NOT RELEASING.

What you're penalised for when you're covered by at least twenty sweaty, hairy bodies and you're doing your best to get rid of the damn ball.

NUMBER EIGHT.

Academically usually the most qualified and intelligent of the forwards. His job is to pick up the ball when a few inches from the line and dive over in a theatrical way.

He can also be seen running in and out of the tail of the line out wishing he'd taken more notice at the tactics briefing.

IT MUST BE TRUE – IT'S IN THE PAPER!

NUTTER.

Someone who believes the TV rugby pundits.

OFFSIDE.

What the backs playing
against your team always are.

OPTIMIST.

Anyone who thinks the referee is going to
penalise his son for stiff-arming, gouging,
groining, headbutting or even something dirty.

OUTSIDE HALF.

This is the glory position - often called 'steand orff' by people who call the game 'ruggah'. Outside halves see themselves as the playmaker - the pivot - the game controller. They come in two types, those that kick too much and those that give the ball out too much.

To attract attention of county or country selectors some outside halves grow their hair long and dye it blond.

I USED TO BE A VET !!

PHYSIOTHERAPIST.

The physio plays a very important part in looking after the players. He or she with gentle healing fingers can coax a wayward hamstring back into life, or dash about offering hangover cures during the close-season tours.

Top clubs have highly qualified physios while those in the lower leagues have to manage with struck-off vets or de-frocked St John Ambulance men doing the job.

EVEN PROPS NEED TO BE LOVED.

PROPS.

These come in pairs, because usually one can read and the other one can write.

Their job is to support the hooker as he strikes snake-like for the ball.

In addition to this props often show an enthusiastic interest in rearranging the faces of the opposing props.

PSYCHO.

Every team has one - he's
the chap, not content
with maiming anyone
not wearing his own
teams colours, he'll
also embarrass the
club during the after-
match hospitality
often by doing a
filthy strip routine or
becoming over-
familiar with the
host club chairman's
wife.

Psychos are usually
studying for a career
in the Church.

AND STOP DRIPPING BLOOD ALL OVER THE CLUB BAR FLOOR

QUACK.

This is the name given to the club's doctor who offers his medical advice to injured players.

However injured, even those players with broken limbs will leap up and run away on seeing the quack approaching, knowing very well that he's probably blind drunk after spending from 11am in the sponsors' hospitality tent.

AND YOU CAN QUOTE ME ON THIS...

QUOTE.

Never believe a quote, particularly the one that says 'Player X figures prominently in my plans for the future of this team.' This is guaranteed to see Player X's contract being chopped.

REFEREES.

He's the chap who's forever stepping in to prevent interesting fights developing. According to touch line fans referees are always born out of wedlock and they also have defective sight.

RETALIATE.

What every self-respecting
player does before his
opponents do it to him!

RUGBY WRITERS.

A well meaning sociable bunch of people.
Some of them ex-players. Rugby writers
when in the press box take a vote to ensure
they all agree who scored that last try.

SECOND ROW.

Usually the biggest chap in the team. Second row players are selected for their great strength, knowledge of tactical scrummaging and repertoire of filthy songs.

Second rows are usually medical students.

SOUTH AFRICA.

The winners of the 1995 World Cup.
A truly great side, hardly ever
beaten - except by Wales.

OOPS, SORRY SIR.

STIFF ARM.

This is not a medical condition, but one of
many dirty tackles a player should have in
his range of tackles. Properly used the
stiff arm tackle can result in ending a
players career and we don't want that, do
we? He may quit the game and become yet
another TV rugby pundit.

T IS FOR...

TRUST ME!

COACH

TACTICS.

What coaches expect players
to remember to do when
they're on the field.

EXCUSE ME REF — YOU MISSED A NAUGHTY THERE

TOUCH JUDGE.

This is the chap on the touch line with a little flag who thinks it's his business if he sees anyone doing naughties on the pitch.

He's forever running on to tell the ref (who never seems to notice these things) and generally spoils the game for everyone. Touch judges used to be school sneaks.

TRAINING.

What the coach expects his players to be doing all the time. It's all very well for World Cup squads - they've got nothing to do in between games. For the average club player training twice a week makes you far too weary to play properly on a Saturday.

U IS FOR..

UNDERDOGS.

Any side playing
the All Blacks.

UNION.

This is the fifteen a side game
as opposed to league which is
played by thirteen men. However,
the object of both games is the
same - hit hell out of whoever's
got the ball.

NEXT, A TOAST —
THE WRU!

UP AND UNDER.

See Gary Owen.

VIOLENCE.

The part of the game the props like best.

VISITORS.

The bunch of players who arrive for a game at your club and are determined to accept as much hospitality, food and drink as they can possibly devour.

THERE WAS A YOUNG LADY OF BARKING CREEK, WHO...

VULGARITY.

A necessary part of post match songs.

WALES.

Without doubt the greatest rugby nation in the world. A nation that truly loves the game. A place where new born babies are given the names of the latest Welsh XV - this is all very well if the baby is a boy, if however…

CROESO Y GYMRU BRING YOUR OWN BOOTS

49

WHINGER.

Usually the visiting team's secretary who at away games moans about the pitch, the hospitality, the 'homer' ref and the facilities.

WINGER.

A wonderful position to play for chatting up the touch-line talent.

Many a winger's concentration has been destroyed by a mini-skirt-clad beauty who in turn was enjoying seeing him in his non regulation too tight shorts.

X.

The unknown quantity or the seconds, as they are sometimes known.

X-RAY.

What happens when your team's psycho tackles the oppositions' assassin.

XENOPHOBIA.

What you didn't know you could be accused of being, until your team play a dirty foreign visiting side.

HELP MUMMY!

YELLOW.

A condition that strikes any player who finds himself the only line of defence between the opposition's nineteen stone of heaving flesh who is even-timing towards him.

SORRY SIR, THEY SEEM TO HAVE DROPPED YOU IN FAVOUR OF ME.

YOUTH PLAYERS.

These are the fresh-faced young athletic enthusiasts who have yet to be slowed down by women, booze and tobacco.

ANYONE GOT THE TOMATO SAUCE?

YUMMY.

The noise a forward makes on tasting an opponent's ear.

ZEALOT..

Usually the coach who's jumping up and down trying to convince you that you can actually beat the world champions, while you're fielding eight from the seconds and several players on work experience.

ZZZ...

A rugby fan watching a really
exciting marathon.